W9-AYE-689

Hello.

THE
HAPPY
BOOK

a journal to celebrate
what makes you happy

Rachel Kempster

Meg Leder

SOURCEBOOKS, INC.®
NAPERVILLE, ILLINOIS

Copyright © 2009 by Rachel Kempster and Meg Leder
Cover and internal design © 2009 by Sourcebooks, Inc.
All entries on pages 7, 33, 55, 74, 75, 103, 125, 149, 172 are courtesy of the individual contributors. Copyright © 2009 of each contributor.
Cover Design by Henry Sene Yee

Sourcebooks and the colophon are registered trademarks of Sourcebooks, Inc.

All rights reserved. No part of this book may be reproduced in any form or by any electronic or mechanical means including information storage and retrieval systems, except in the case of brief quotations embodied in critical articles or reviews, without permission in writing from its publisher, Sourcebooks, Inc.

Art on pages 191, 154, 169, 104, 156, 113, 82, 115, 50, 176, 39, 139, 165 courtesy of Norn Cutson. Copyright © 2009, Norn Cutson.
Art on pages 46, 10, 80 courtesy of Steven Leder. Copyright © 2009, Steven Leder.
Art on pages 170, 171 courtesy of Megan Mitchell. Copyright © 2009, Megan Mitchell.
Art on page 155 courtesy of Corrine Doron. Copyright © 2009, Corrinne Doron.
Art on page 159 courtesy of Gabiel Fynsk. Copyright © 2009, Gabriel Fynsk.
Art on pages 136, 40, 24 courtesy of Christopher Lackner. Copyright © 2009, Christopher Lackner.
Art on pages 92, 93, 27 courtesy of Megan Patrick. Copyright © 2009, Megan Patrick.
Art on page 65 courtesy of Ben Gibson. Copyright © 2009, Ben Gibson.
Art on pages 177, 127 courtesy of Phoebe Collins and Matt Collins. Copyright © 2009, Phoebe Collins and Matt Collins.
Art on page 144 courtesy of Sarah Hayes. Copyright © 2009, Sarah Hayes.
Art on page 69 courtesy of Vince Venditti. Copyright © 2009, Vince Venditti.

All brand names and product names used in this book are trademarks, registered trademarks, or trade names of their respective holders. Sourcebooks, Inc., is not associated with any product or vendor in this book.

Published by Sourcebooks, Inc.
P.O. Box 4410, Naperville, Illinois 60567-4410
(630) 961-3900
Fax: (630) 961-2168
www.sourcebooks.com

Printed and bound in the United States of America.
VP 10 9 8 7 6 5 4

To Candace,
who started it all.

And to Donovan, Clara,
Delaney, and Jack,
who make us happy.

INTRODUCTION

"Subtly, in the little ways, joy has been leaking out of our lives. The small pleasures of the ordinary day seem almost contemptible, and glance off us lightly.... Perhaps it's a good time to reconsider pleasure at its roots. Changing out of wet shoes and socks, for instance. Bathrobes. Yawning and stretching. Real tomatoes."

—*Barbara Holland*

What makes you happy? Maybe it's:

- Fresh-grated Parmesan cheese
- Making your brother laugh
- Feeling it get dark outside
- Finding chairs in the garbage
- The shine of wet leaves
- A willful cat that will sit on your lap, no matter what

The Happy Book is about celebrating what makes you glad, what gives you joy from your heart down to the tips of your toes, what makes you quietly appreciative and full inside, or what makes you feel just dang content.

That stuff can be hard to find. Every day, we practice new skills on the job and at school so we can learn and improve. We engage in exercises so we can get in shape and stay healthy. We work at being social so we can play well with others and function in society. But we don't practice happiness. When we experience feeling happy, it's amazing and beautiful, but fleeting. We don't know how to tap into it at will.

Imagine being able to tap into that happy rhythm. Imagine working your happy muscle so you have it at the ready. Imagine cultivating it and growing happiness, so you have a garden of joy in front of you. Imagine whatever mixed metaphor you want, as long as it has cultivating happiness as the result.

That's what this book will teach you to do—to practice happiness so it gets easier to find.

The Happy Book gives you the opportunity to create a living record of the things in life—friends, memories, family, foods, books, songs, quotes, ideas, dreams—that make you happy. You'll scribble, sketch, ponder, paste, doodle, and play. You'll make this book your own.

In the end, you'll have worked your happy muscles, grown that garden of joy, tapped the melody that gives you bliss. You'll have created happy.

HOW TO USE YOUR HAPPY BOOK

The quick answer is, "Use it however you want, as long as it makes you happy." But if you're the type of person who likes your ducks in a row before you start any project, here are some thoughts to get you started:

- Use your book when you feel happy. It's no small thing to be happy, and when it happens, we need to hold on to it as long as we can. Writing about it helps you bottle up its essence like dandelion wine.
- Pick it up when you feel crappy. If your day has just been ridiculously, stupidly awful, and you are done trying to make the best of it, no need to write in the book—just read it.
- It's OK to skip around the book. There's no special order.
- If you don't like what's on the page, cross it out and rewrite it in a way you like, even if it's just making room for a grocery list or a letter to a crush or scribbling. This is your book, and it's about what makes *you* happy.
- A lot of the prompts are open. This means you can respond however you'd like. Make a list. Paste in pictures. Draw your answer. Fill it in on different days. Write upside down.
- No amending or editing what you wrote later on. You're going for what makes you happy in the present moment. You have to respect what made an earlier, younger version of yourself happy (even if it's *You've Got Mail*, a movie you now detest).

- Don't worry about spelling and grammar, or what other people think about your thoughts. Tell that inner editor to go take a vacation to Barcelona where it can chill and drink hot chocolate with churros while you spend time with your book, making as many spelling errors as you dang well please.
- There's a certain joy that can come from being arbitrary and embracing your own quirks. Create a completely arbitrary rule for your book (e.g., "If someone has eaten a pickle today, they can't write in the book until they read some Dr. Seuss." "I will only write in my book after I've listened to Bonnie Tyler's 'I Need a Hero.'" "If you like Tom Hanks, you can't write in my book.") and write it here:

_____

_____

The Moral of the Story, the Authors' Manifesto, the Theme to This Book, *The Happy Book's* Happy Ending, the Secret for Happiness…

Thinking about what makes you happy, makes you happy.
Writing about what makes you happy, makes you happy.
Reading about what makes you happy, makes you happy.
Asking others to think, read, and write about what makes them happy, makes them happy. The nice side effect? It also makes you happy.

ONCE UPON A TIME...

When I was in college, I asked my friend Candace, who was going through a stressful time, to make a list of ten things to be happy about. After number sixty ("Having cool gold rings that make your fingers look all slim and svelte"), we kept the list going and asked friends and family, baristas, and other coffee shop patrons to add to the list. Four notebooks later, we have over 3600 entries and a coffee-stained, weathered, and marvelous chronicle of things that bring us joy.

— *Meg*

Make a list of things that make you happy—anything and everything that makes you happy—small, big, profound, simple.

GRANDMAS, DOGS, AND RAINBOWS

There are certain unspoken associations of happiness: cookie-baking grandmas, faithful childhood dogs, a sky full of rainbows. But just because lots of people love something doesn't mean it's wrong for you to love it too. Pick your favorite happy cliché, and write about it here.

In an episode of the TV show *Gossip Girl*, a young girl told the character Blair Waldorf, "But you're perfect!" Blair's response? "True."

Whether you're a fan or not, there's something to be said for celebrating yourself and singing yourself, for giving voice to your inner Blair Waldorf. Find at least three things that you really like about yourself, whether it's your near-perfect handwriting, your long eyelashes, or your ability to stand on one leg for an extraordinary amount of time. Write them here. Shamelessly brag about yourself. Quiz your friends on your list, until they can recite it too. Celebrate yourself, and sing yourself.

"I celebrate myself, and sing myself."

—*Walt Whitman*

AFFIRMATION CELEBRATION

This isn't as new-agey as it sounds. Create an affirmation wallet card and take the good vibes with you everywhere you go.

Cut an index card to roughly the same size as a credit card (i.e., wallet-sized). Or, use the templates provided on the next page.

On your card, write at least one really nice thing about yourself ("Meg, your nose has character."). Or write the three things you like the best about yourself (see p. 3). Or write an uber-positive saying ("Click your heels three times and say: 'I can't stand how gorgeous I am.'").

You can laminate your card with laminating sheets (found at any office-supply store), or you can even ask the store to laminate it for you. Carry your affirmation card in your wallet with your library card.

Play hooky from work or school! Just do it. Paste in your souvenirs from your day off.

Spontaneous Happiness Generator!

The first snowfall of the year, finding money in your coat from last year, warm towels out of the dryer that smell like fabric softener, unexpected post cards in the mail, watching movies with my niece and nephew, and listening to Bon Jour

Jaimie

The BRUMPH! of plane tires announcing my return home. Brml

Saturday afternoon cuddles with a sweetie and a dog- Lance

- My new bike
- Video games
- macaroni and cheese
- Singing in the shower
- getting tickled
  Donovan

freshly laundered sheets. - Jess

When there are equal amounts of each color in my bag of M+M's - Craig

When my 1½ yr old grandson says 'Papa Papa' and hugs me like a long lost buddy - PAPA Jim

Glittery and sparkly items? Collect them like a bird building a nest—with an eye for shiny things and a willingness to put them all together willy-nilly. Paste 'em here.

If you're familiar with *A Light in the Attic*, *Where the Sidewalk Ends*, *The Missing Piece*, and other Shel Silverstein books, you know that he is a master of the silly but poignant rhyme, and that he has awesome poems about picking one's nose, bears living in refrigerators, and the perils of not taking out the garbage. If you're not familiar with his work, it's time to start (www.shelsilverstein.com).

Write your favorite Shel Silverstein poem here, and then try and memorize it.

Who are your favorite people in the world? List them here:

"I have learned that to be with those I like is enough."

—*Walt Whitman*

Your Own Happy Pages:

Fill in whatever manner you wish.

What's your favorite thing? Cats? Reading? Sleeping in? Shakespeare? Find a bunch of happy quotes about it and write them here.

Head on over to GoogleMaps (http://maps.google.com) and create your own personalized happy map of the all the countries, cities, and streets that mean the world to you.

Print it out and paste a copy here.

Here are a few ideas to get you started:

- Mark your favorite childhood locales—from your elementary school to the site of your first kiss.
- Note your favorite vacation spots—from your family trip to Yosemite to your honeymoon in Bali.

GUEST SCRIBBLE

Every day, you see the same people—colleagues, classmates, your bus driver, your neighbor. Find one of those people—someone you see every day,
but don't know well at all—and invite him or her to write a list of a few things
that make him or her happy—right here, right now, in this book.

Feeling sheepish? Visit writeinmyjournal.com for inspiration.

BUILD A STORY

On a road trip, my friends Curt, Brian, and I stopped to listen to some blues music in Louisville, Kentucky. Fueled by the music and visiting a new place, and being awake in the wee hours after midnight, we started with the line, "Once upon a time, there was a bald boxer named Sam…" and took turns writing different lines to a story. In the end, after mishaps, missed connections, and a shared dinner of General Tso's chicken, Sam the bald boxer ended up marrying his longtime love, Lucy the librarian, in front of Hagia Sophia.

Now it's your turn.

— *Meg*

Come up with the most odd, cryptic, or ridiculous scenario you can imagine, and write it as the first line of the story in the space below. Pass the book to a friend to write the next line. After that, share it with another friend to write the third line, and so on. Enlist as many friends as you want. Once everyone's written a line, write another line, and pass it around again. The only rules? Build the story in new and unexpected ways. The weirder, wackier, and more ridiculous, the better.

If you need help getting started, try the prompts below:

- You go to the grocery store and realize all the food has been replaced by toasters.
- You bring home a kitten from the animal shelter and learn it speaks perfect English.
- Once upon a time, there was a girl named Kyra who wanted to create a magical roller skating rink.

Whether it's "Shiny Happy People" by REM, "Birdhouse in Your Soul" by They Might Be Giants, or "Sweet Caroline" by Neil Diamond, some songs just make you glad. Start a list of happy songs here. Try to add a new song every week. Ask your friends to contribute.

A few years ago, Meg and I were on a sock-monkey making kick. Our friend Carol joined in the fun and we spent a long day turning red-heeled socks into silly plush monkeys. The next day Meg and I both received a surprise in the mail—Carol sent us something called Anti-Monkey-Butt Powder, a bottle of powder featuring a goofy cartoon monkey on the label. I laughed for days just thinking about it.

—*Rachel*

Send someone a completely unexpected and silly present. A box of Thin Mints, a bottle of Anti-Monkey-Butt Powder, seeds to grow daisies, a dollar-store tchotchke, or scratch-and-sniff stickers. Anything that will catch the recipient by surprise and make him smile for days.

In the movie *Smoke*, Harvey Keitel's character takes a picture of the same street block at the same time, day after day, year after year. He creates an album of these moments, with seasons and people moving in and out of them. Pick a particular time on a particular day of the week and, every week, list what makes you most happy at that specific moment, until you fill up these two pages. Watch your moments of joy accumulate, shift, and circle back in again.

Clue, Ghost in the Graveyard, Hungry Hungry Hippo, reenacting scenes from *Little House on the Prairie*... what were your favorite games to play when you were a kid? Doesn't matter if they came in a box or from your imagination.

"Unplug for a day." I'll admit that it didn't initially sound like the happiest idea to a happily plugged-in girl like me. But I did it, and now I'm a believer! I spent a weekend away from TV and the Interwebs… and it rocked. I tried out new recipes, caught up on a stack of magazines and books, and sent out some long overdue thank-you notes. As a bonus, I loved my computer even more when I plugged it back in on Monday.

—Rachel

How would you spend an unplugged day? Plan it here and then DO IT!

GET MESSY, MAKE PLAYDOUGH!

It's hard to resist the temptation of playdough. Whip yourself up a batch from scratch (a quick Google search will yield hundreds of quick and easy recipes) or pick up a few containers of the real thing. Then go to town! How can you be anything less than happy while squeezing a bright, shiny ball of playdough between your fingers?

10 fun, joy-making things to do with playdough:

- The smell of playdough is unmistakable. Try to describe it on this page.
- Make a snowman. Then smash him.
- Make a big pile of snakes by rolling small balls of dough between your hand and the table.
- Sculpt yourself out of playdough. Embellish with buttons, yarn, and any other craft supplies you have around the house. Take a picture of your finished sculpture and paste it here (and use it as your profile pic on the social networking sites you frequent).
- Invite over a friend and have a playdough war. Throw it. Get it stuck in your hair.
- Spell your name out in playdough. Spell your cat's name in playdough.
- Make a garden full of playdough flowers.
- Have a sculpture contest at your next party.
- Make fake food out of playdough—fake pizza, fake donuts, fake sushi.
- Give playdough to a friend who's having a rough day.

REGISTER SURPRISES

Our friend Jenny loves taking a potential purchase to a cashier only to find out it's actually unexpectedly on sale. She calls the lucky moment a "Register Surprise." What lucky moments have surprised you? Running into an old friend when you're on vacation…being the tenth caller and winning Depeche Mode tickets or a Jefferson Starship album…winning lunch for your office when your business card is plucked out of the Free Lunch jar at Chipotle…List them here.

Good
Luck

Write your favorite smells here.

Toast

Cinnamon

Fall leaves

Clean laundry

Write your favorite sounds here.

A revving engine

Your niece saying your name

Kittens purring

The ice cream truck

What's your favorite color? Fill these pages with different iterations of it...Do you like green? Stick on some grass. Do you live for yellow? Find your favorite shades on paint chips at the hardware store and tape them here. Red? Find every related shade of Crayola and scribble away.

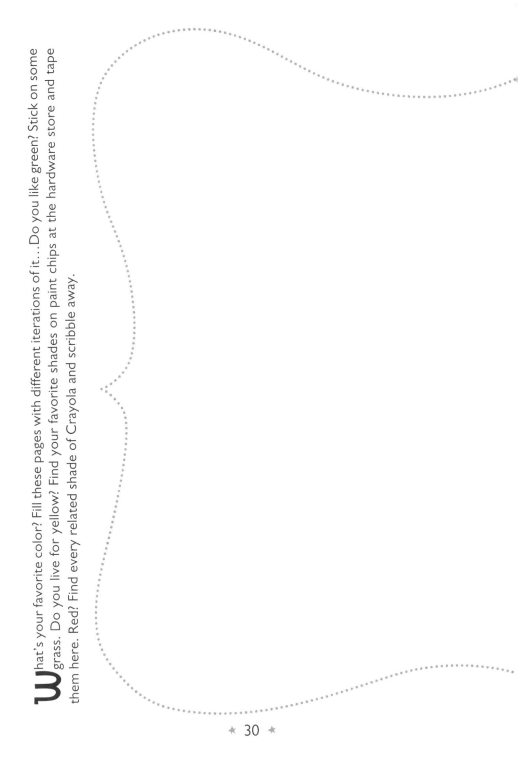

HAPPY BULLETIN BOARD

I go to San Diego Comic Con (an annual celebration of everything comics and pop culture) every year, and it's one of my favorite happy places on the planet. This year I came home with lots of joy-bringing swag, including big bright Tokidoki stickers, a 501st Legion pin, and a paper Cylon mask from *Battlestar Galactica*. These treasures definitely didn't fit into my 4 x 6-inch happy book, but I couldn't bear to hide them away...so for a month they sat in a neat happy pile on my bookshelf. Then I had an idea—in my office at work I had a big old bulletin board filled with good things, like thank-you notes, pictures of my favorite people, even a felt pennant for days when I need a little rah rah rah. Why not do the same for at home? I found an oversized cork board at an office supply store and stocked up on push pins. Now I've got a big tribute to all the things I love right smack in the middle of my living room. Why not give it a whirl yourself?

—Rachel

Here are some other ideas for filling up your own happy bulletin board:

- Blow up a few of your favorite photos into 8 x 10s.
- Tack up old broken necklaces, buttons, and anything else that adds some sparkle and shine.
- Act like a teenager and post up some photos of your favorite rock stars.
- Do you have a big day coming up? Or do you just love Christmas? Keep a countdown going on your happy board.
- Print out a personal happy mantra or repeat one of your happy affirmations (see p. 4) in giant type.

Spontaneous Happiness Generator!

Playing a mix of guilty pleasures 80's songs in the car and singing along at the _top_ of my lungs. (madonna, anyone?! ☺)

Lilly

SCORING A STACK OF GREAT LIBRARY BOOKS AND HAVING HOURS OF UNINTERRUPTED TIME TO PLOW THROUGH THEM! — Amy

Picnic in the park

Travis

A fully-stocked refrigerator — Erin

Laughing to the point of tears; dancing & kissing; new adventures _and_ fish & chips with Guinness! ★Megan

Being with the family during the holidays! Harry

HAND TURKEY

For many of us, the times we've felt the happiest making things were back in kindergarten—before we worried if what we were doing was "right" or "looked good." Rediscover some of that joy by going for a traditional kindergarten craft: the hand turkey. Trace your hands on these pages and decorate those turkeys with abandon—crayons, glitter, feathers. Don't worry—it's hard to mess up a hand turkey when there's no wrong way to do it.

Your Own Happy Pages: Fill in whatever manner you wish.

Describe your perfect Sunday.

Describe your perfect sundae.

Napoleon Dynamite loves a good liger. Now it's time to channel your inner zoologist (or, rather, cryptozoologist) and create an animal hybrid. Draw a picture of your rabbihippo, toucanosaurus, bearicorn, or catigator here.

Note: This works especially well if you're a terrible artist.

What things have you accomplished that, prior to finishing, you were dreading to the depths of your soul? Going to the dentist after a three-year "hiatus"? Reading all one hundred books for your master's exam? Here's your spot to list those things, then cross them off. It's OK that you've already done them—you need to celebrate striking the big things off your to-do list.

Consider adding things you still need to do. You can draw inspiration from seeing them next to a list of all the other things you've accomplished.

PHOTO SCAVENGER HUNT

Get your friends involved in a fun photo scavenger hunt.

1. Come up with a list of ten to twenty adjectives and objects. Anything from green to dinner to circle to crazy to sneakers—the less restrictive the words, the more fun and varied the results.
2. Email your friends the list, tell them what you're doing, and give them a deadline. Let them know they each have to photograph every item on the list.
3. Ask everyone to upload their photos to a service like Flickr where you can easily share your results.
4. When all the photos are in, ask everyone to vote on the winners in each category—just for kicks—and then announce the winners (over email is fun, but in an ice cream store would be more fun).
5. Post all your favorite photos here—and then plan for the next hunt.

What's your absolute favorite recipe? Copy it here.

SENIOR SUPERLATIVES

Use this page to assign happy superlatives to your friends. Best hair? Prettiest handwriting? Most likely to marry Bon Jovi? Dorkiest laugh? The sillier and weirder the better.

"It was a quiet morning, the town covered over with darkness and at ease in bed. Summer gathered in the weather, the wind had the proper touch, the breathing of the world was long and warm and slow. You had only to rise, lean from your window, and know that this indeed was the first real time of freedom and living, this was the first morning of summer."

—*Ray Bradbury*, Dandelion Wine

As a kid, what did summer vacation mean to you? The anticipation of three delicious months of sleeping in, swimming, catching fireflies, playing Kick the Can, and eating popsicles? List your favorite summer rituals here.

For me, the taste of summer is a root beer float from the Root Beer Stand in Sharonville, Ohio, where I grew up. The stand opens in the spring, when the weather starts to warm up again, and their homemade root beer is delicious and amazing and June/July/August all rolled into one. So in the dead of winter, when I need a taste of summer and Ohio, and I don't have easy access to either, I make a root beer float.

— *Meg*

How to make a root beer float in the dead of winter:

1. Put a mug in the freezer until it's frosted.
2. In the meantime, put on some summertime music: "In the Summertime" by Mungo Jerry, "Free Fallin'" by Tom Petty and the Heartbreakers, "California Stars" by Wilco and Billy Bragg, "In the Sun" by Blondie, "Summer Nights (Summer Lovin')" by John Travolta & Olivia Newton-John, "The Summer Wind" by Madeline Peyroux, and any of the songs called "Summertime" by The Sundays, DJ Jazzy Jeff and the Fresh Prince (yep), Ella Fitzgerald, Billie Holiday, Sarah Vaughan, or Janis Joplin.
3. Once the mug is chilled to your liking, fill the cup halfway with root beer.
4. Add one scoop of vanilla ice cream.
5. Drizzle some root beer on top to get a proper foam—there may be some overflow, so be prepared to start drinking immediately.
6. Pretend you're sitting outside in the sun and enjoy.

Paste your favorite pictures of yourself here.

Some say it's a bad idea to bring baked goods into work. Phooey. Everyone loves gooey, homemade cookies. Whip up a batch. Oatmeal raisin? Chocolate chunk? Plain old sugar? Try out different cookie cutter shapes. Consider icing your creations, and go wild with sprinkles and food coloring.

Share the scrumptious results with friends, co-workers, the mailmen, your favorite check-out chick at the supermarket, or anyone else who looks like they need a tasty taste of happiness. Use this space to record your cookie-giving exploits.

Remember how glorious it was to make a mess when you were a kid? It's time to let your inner creative artist out with finger paint. You can find finger paint at most craft stores. Cover your work space with newspaper. Find a piece of poster board, and fill it with sloppy, glorious art. Then paste a corner of the result here.

Every now and then, you come across a sentence or two in a book that makes you gasp or laugh or wish you had written it…

What are the sentences you wish you had written? Find your favorite passages and record them here.

"Her clocks ached. Time had congealed."

—*Charles Baxter*, "The Cures for Love," *Believers*

"Through the window they saw a light rain of tiny yellow flowers falling. They fell on the town all through the night in a silent storm, and they covered the roof and blocked the doors and smothered the animals who slept outdoors. So many flowers fell from the sky that in the morning the streets were carpeted with a compact cushion and they had to clear them away with shovels and rakes."

—Gabriel García Márquez, 100 Years of Solitude

What things bring you comfort? Hands around a warm coffee mug, a cat purring in your lap, your mom's rice pudding. List them here.

"There must be quite a few things that a hot bath won't cure, but I don't know many of them."

— Sylvia Plath

Spontaneous Happiness Generator!

it makes me happy to make others happy
I know that sounds so cornball but its true
.... & I get really frustrated when I don't!

Tea parties with my granddaughter — a cup of
sugar water, graham crackers + a sweet
little girl. — Pat (Nana)

PURPLE
        POPSICLES   CLARA

Peppermint anything during Christmas time -
ice cream, cocoa, anything!
                        Anne

        Baking as an act of love. — Katherine

watching Mary Tyler Moore show re-runs!
                        Susan

    My hilarious friends!! — Meredith

Create the perfect guest list for the most perfect dinner party you can imagine. Let nothing—time, budget, space, or reasonableness—limit you. On the seating chart, place your grandma next to Elvis. Include Aristotle alongside your beloved kindergarten teacher. Add more seats if you wish. And plan your menu, with, of course, eight courses of dessert.

Menu

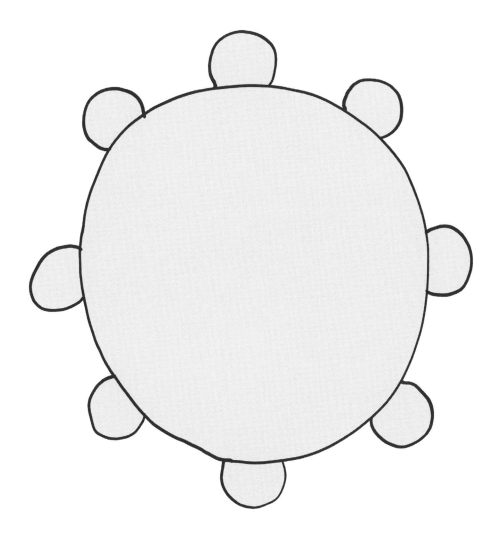

List your favorite happy movies here. You can even break them down into categories—Favorite Movies from Childhood, Funniest Movies, Sad Movies with the Happiest of Endings, Guilty Pleasures.

YOUR PAGE FOR LISTING YOUR FAVORITE JOKES

Instructions for telling one of the most satisfying jokes ever:

1. Say, "Knock knock" to a friend.
2. When they ask, "Who's there?" say, "Impatient cow."
3. When they begin to say, "Impatient cow who?" interrupt and yell, "Moo!"

Your Own Happy Pages: Fill in whatever manner you wish.

My ex-boyfriend has the coolest grandma in the universe. Grandma Sylvia taught me to be a kinder, gentler, stronger human being. She also gave me two very specific pieces of advice: 1. Don't put off until tomorrow what you can do today, and 2. Don't leave the house with dirty shoes.

It's been over ten years since Grandma imparted that advice to me, but it really stuck with me. Scuffed shoes bother me as much as they bothered her. And I try my hardest not to procrastinate about things big (telling someone I love them) or small (getting the dishes done before I go to bed).

And right here and now I'd like to send a hearty, warm THANK YOU to Grandma Sylvia for giving me a gift better than my own pony or a giant ruby ring—the tools and advice I needed to develop self-respect.

—*Rachel*

The best gifts are often intangible. Maybe it was a boy who shared with you his love for The Cure. Or your grandma, who taught you how to knit. Who gave you a taste for Thai or introduced you to the fine art of karaoke? Identify a few of these intangible gifts, and write thank-you notes to the people who introduced or gave them to you—whether they know it or not.

In the old TV show *Rudolph the Red-Nosed Reindeer*, Hermey the elf hates making toys and just wants to be a dentist—not exactly a popular occupation for an elf. What unpopular things make you happy? Maybe it's doing the dishes or preparing your tax return or sitting in traffic. What do you surprisingly but wholeheartedly really dig?

"We should all do what, in the long run, gives us joy, even if it is only picking grapes or sorting the laundry."

—*E. B. White*

What are your favorite types of fireworks? The ones that look like tadpoles? Sea anemones? The simple but awesome sparkler? Draw them or paste photos of them here. Make the page explode with fireworks.

I used to work at an ice cream store in Sharonville, Ohio, named Sharondippety. I applied solely because I loved the name, but I also grew to love the art of making waffle cones, coming up with good sundae combinations, and developing a well-muscled "dipping arm" from scooping so much deliciousness. To this day, the name of the place still makes me very happy.

— Meg

Spend some time with an atlas, or the Yellow Pages, or your own experience, and list the happiest-sounding places you can find: Papabubble, Mooncake Foods, 12 Chairs, Scarlett O' Hair-a...

"Will you please call me Cordelia?" she asked eagerly.

"Call you Cordelia! Is that your name?"

"No-o-o, it's not exactly my name, but I would love to be called Cordelia. It's such a perfectly elegant name."

—*L. M. Montgomery*, Anne of Green Gables

Here's your page to list all the names you admire or wish you had been named.

CREATURE MAKER

Sometimes happiness can come from the ugliest things. Be a creature maker. Invite a few friends over, crack open a bottle of wine, and craft the ugliest monster you can possibly fashion. Give him or her a ridiculously sweet name, as well as a history and life story. Make it loved.

If you need some inspiration, visit the CRAFT website (http://blog. craftzine.com) and search for "monster" or "creature."

Very easy creature recipe:

Supplies

- Two sheets of felt (cheap felt, fancy felt, homemade felt—felt of any kind!)
- Embroidery thread in a complimentary color
- Scissors
- A marker
- A file folder (or a piece of cardboard)
- Stuffing
- Buttons, bits of yarn, scrap fabric, beads—and any other bits and bobs you've got hanging around

Instructions

1. Draw a simple shape for your creature on the file folder/cardboard. If you're a novice crafter, stick to a simple shape for your monster like a square or a rectangle. If you're a comfortable crafter, you can choose a more adventurous shape. Use a copier to blow up these templates 200% (or any size that will work with your felt).
2. Cut out your template. Trace it onto the felt twice.
3. You now have the front and back of your creature cut out of the felt. Sweet! Now, you need to sew the two halves together. Put the two pieces on top of each other. Make sure that the "bad sides"—the side of the felt with the marker trace line—are facing out.
4. Sew the two sides together. If you're an excellent seamstress, you'll make tiny perfect stitches. If you're like me, you'll do the best you can. Be sure to leave a 1–2 inch hole unsewn.

5. Flip your creature right-side out through the unsewn hole. Fill the creature with stuffing. Chopsticks are handy if you're stuffing long and skinny arms or legs or other bits.
6. Sew the stuffing hole closed.
7. Make a face using buttons, markers, embroidery thread, and anything else you have on hand.

List as many moments of happiness as you can find from today and today only. Right here, now. Fill the page. As the esteemed Tim Gunn would say, "Make it work."

"She lay back, and all was light and warmth. Life, she thought, is sometimes sad and often dull, but there are currants in the cake and here is one of them."

—*Nancy Mitford*, The Pursuit of Love

What's your favorite vacation memory? Whether it's a trip to Costa Rica or a childhood visit to a theme park, write about it here. What smells do you remember? What new foods did you try? What things did you do and see? Do you have a picture from the vacation? Paste it here.

"To awaken quite alone in a strange town is one of the pleasantest sensations in the world."

—Freya Stark

Learn how to compliment people in another language, but make sure the compliments are unique and quirky and slightly crazy. Yahoo! Babelfish plus your imagination equals a world of fun new things to say. Here are some to get you started. List more here.

- Yo amo lo que has hecho a tu casa. ("I love what you have done to your house" in Spanish.)
- Chaussures intéressantes! ("Nice shoes!" in French.)
- Avete spalle belle. ("You have lovely shoulders" in Italian.)
- U bent mijn zonneschijn, mijn enige zonneschijn. ("You are my sunshine, my only sunshine" in Dutch.)

HAPPY HAIKU

The beauty of haiku comes from being economical with your words—you're forced to describe things as simply as possible (first line: five syllables, second line: seven syllables, last line: five syllables), and in the process, you find new ways of thinking and describing. Write a series of haikus about your favorite things.

"Haiku for Leonardo DiCaprio"
by Meg

Jack Dawson, so good,
I wish you were my boyfriend,
You take care of trees.

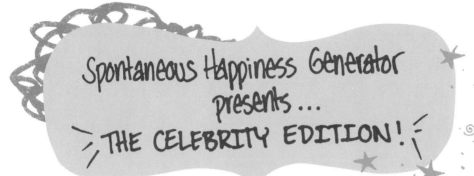

Hear from our favorite authors, thinkers, cooks, designers, inspire-ers, and people we admire... oooh!

Watching the snow fall and not having anywhere to get to.
— Charles Baxter

Theme Restaurants, Pie, Amusement Park Water Stunt Shows, Point Break, Haunted Mansions and Pharmaceutical Pens.

WAKING UP EVERY MORNING AND LOOKING AT TREES. —KERI SMITH

BEING THE FIRST ONE IN THE KITCHEN — RICHARD BLAIS

Spending hours lost in the stacks at the Strand bookstore...
Jessica Queller

...at moment when you walk into a party, when no one has spotted you yet, and u can just take a moment to watch your friends laugh and enjoy each other's company.

Cat Deeley

Shiny Stuff. Cute little dogs that make me go "Aw!" And a Delicious cocktail with a good friend.

FRANCESCO Sotta

Something that makes me happy

THE OLD-SCHOOL TV. ADS FOR THE DETROIT ZOO!!

"My lines, my lines, I can't remember my lines!!"

check 'em out on YouTube!

Davy Rothbart

The soft spot behind a dog's ears. That's what dreams are made of! *Kembri Cruz*

Smelling my wife's morning breath while she is still in bed—especially when she doesn't want me to! *David Roche*

my dog Harry -MIZRAHI

Sometimes the book is too good to put down. Be an irresponsible adult and stay up all night finishing a brilliant book—*Superfudge* (it's hilarious!), *The Ruins* (it's really scary!), *Love in the Time of Cholera* (it's quirkily romantic), *The Likeness* (it's thrilling!), *Spud* (it's cheeky!), *Holidays on Ice* (it's dang funny! Better than *Cats*!)—or playing a mesmerizing video game, or watching *Buffy the Vampire Slayer*, season two. In the wee hours of the night, write here about what it's like to be awake when everyone else is sleeping.

Go outside and get some sunshine. While you're out there soaking it all in, doodle all kinds of sunshiny prettiness here.

Families are an intricate machine made of shared history, love, tradition, weirdness, and comfort. Post your favorite family photos here. What elements of the Happiness Machine are at work?

"'Sure,' he murmured. 'There it is.' And he watched with now-gentle sorrow and now-quick delight, and at last quiet acceptance as all the bits and pieces of this house mixed, stirred, settled, poised, and ran steadily again. 'The Happiness Machine,' he said. 'The Happiness Machine.'"

—*Ray Bradbury*, Dandelion Wine

In *Leaves of Grass*, Walt Whitman writes, "A mouse is miracle enough." What little things in nature are miracle enough? The pattern of frost on your window? The veins on a leaf? A blade of grass? Make Walt proud, and list them here.

you're never too old for stickers. Fill this page with stickers that make you happy.

What books did you love as a child? List them here, and then find them to read again. (If you weren't a reader as a kid, consider exploring the amazing world of kids' literature now…the books are simply amazing, which makes us happy.) Here are some of our faves to get you started: *Where the Wild Things Are*; *Harriet the Spy*; *Lily's Purple Plastic Purse*; *Alexander and the Terrible, Horrible, No Good, Very Bad Day*; *The Book Thief*; *The Last Slice of the Rainbow*.

Be a passionate fan for a day. Attend a comic book convention, a pickle festival, a dog show—any place filled with people who find joy in a shared thing. Post pictures and souvenirs here.

"If I am lukewarm about the dahlia, I am red hot about the bearded iris."

—*Katherine White*

Take $10 and buy something completely frivolous that will make you happy. Paste the receipt here. Ideas include:

- $10 of marshmallows
- $10 on a chair massage at a street fair
- $10 on a slice of pie a la mode and coffee at a good restaurant
- $10 on pretty pencils

99.9 percent of Web videos are terrible. But now and again, a diamond appears amid all that coal. We're always struck by funny animal clips and watch them over and over. Since that online joy is fleeting, use this page to track the videos that make you laugh until you cry.

Date:
Description..
Who sent it? ....
Who did you forward it to? ....
Why does it make you happy? ....

Date:
Description..
Who sent it? ....
Who did you forward it to? ....
Why does it make you happy? ....

Date:
Description..
Who sent it? ....
Who did you forward it to? ....
Why does it make you happy? ....

Date:
Description..
Who sent it? ....
Who did you forward it to? ....
Why does it make you happy? ....

Date:
Description..
Who sent it? ....
Who did you forward it to? ....
Why does it make you happy? ....

Draw portraits of your best friends here—even and especially if you're not an artist.

In high school I worked at a fast food restaurant on nights and weekends. I was a cashier, a French-fryer, a strawberry-sundae-maker, and I had a heck of a lot of fun. One quiet Sunday my co-workers engaged in a breakfast-eating contest. For three hours they ate and ate and ate until they could eat no more. There was cheering, gleeful screaming, and a winner proclaimed at the end of the shift. It's such a silly, inconsequential memory, but it's mine.

—Rachel

What are your favorite work memories? The day you worked your first shift as a babysitter and got the kids to bed right on time? The day you finally got an office with a door that closes? Whatever the memory, whatever the job, jot down your favorite memory here.

THE HAPPIEST MEALS

In my office we get awfully bored with our brought-from-home lunches. Jaimie brings bread for her never-ending jar of peanut butter. Vince and Sarah bring last night's dinner. I cobble together what I can from the vending machine. To make things more interesting, I came up with a few ideas to make the midday meal more fun for everyone.

—Rachel

- Make a bento box. In Japan, lunch is an art. You can make your own bento-style lunch for yourself (and your friends) with the same artistic flourishes. Google "bento box" for inspiration, and before you know it you'll be shaping rice into star shapes and adding amazing flourishes to your leftover spaghetti.
- Bring dessert! Buy it or bake it—no one will mind. Be sure to bring enough for the crowd.
- Share your leftovers. Did your veggie lasagna turn out amazing? Text your lunch buddies and tell them NOT to bring in lunch the next day.
- Organize a potluck. Have everyone bring in their very best potluck dish.
- Run with a theme. When tomatoes are in season, challenge everyone to bring in their favorite tomato dish.

Your Own Happy Pages: Fill in whatever manner you wish.

What words make you happy?
Here are some of our favorites:

pumpkin

cattery

lollipop

frazzled

wow

serendipity

Now it's your turn:

STACHE ATTACK

What words make you laugh?

Our faves:

fancy pants

Bob Loblaw

poppycock

poop deck

discombobulate

Anastasia Beaverhausen

kerfuffle

Your turn:

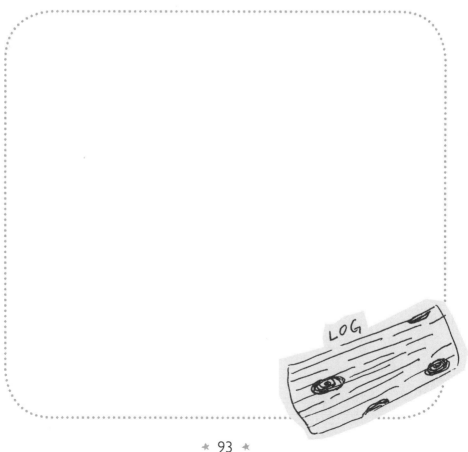

LOG

Every other Thursday, our friend Jessica makes a cake to share at work. All homemade, all delicious, the cakes bring together a group of very happy colleagues, all eager to sample the day's specialty. Consider beginning your own Cake Thursday. And maybe you can start with Jessica's Sunday Cake…a perfect cake for a Thursday!

Sunday Cake

By Jessica Reed

Named as such because it is the type of simple cake I imagine would have been served after Sunday dinner in the Victorian Era

Ingredients
  1 ¾ cups (7.7 ounces) all-purpose flour, spooned and leveled
  2 tsp. baking powder
  ¼ tsp. salt
  ½ cup whole milk
  1 ½ tsp. pure vanilla extract
  1 tsp. orange flower water *(It sounds exotic, but most grocery stores carry the good, yet inexpensive Monteux brand.)*
  1 cup of light brown sugar, packed
  The zest of 1 medium-sized orange or lemon (whichever you prefer)
  1 stick (4 ounces) of unsalted butter, at room temperature
  3 large eggs at room temperature

Instructions
(Note: the recipe is written for a stand mixer, but can easily be done with a hand mixer, or even by hand. If using a hand mixer, follow the instructions below. To do by hand, use muscle power and a whisk, and add an extra minute or two mixing time on to the fifth and sixth steps.)

1. Preheat the oven to 350 degrees.
2. Butter and flour a 9" round cake pan, then place a round of parchment paper (available at most grocery stores) on the bottom and butter the paper.

3. Whisk together the flour, baking powder, and salt in a medium-sized bowl. Set aside.

4. Measure the whole milk in a glass measuring cup, then whisk in the vanilla extract and orange flower water. Set aside.

5. In the bowl of a stand mixer fitted with the paddle attachment, mix up the brown sugar and orange or lemon zest with your fingers, rubbing the zest into the sugar for 15–20 seconds or until wonderfully fragrant. Add the butter to the bowl and cream on medium-high speed for about 3–4 minutes or until you have pale, fluffy concoction.

6. Add the eggs one at a time, mixing on medium speed for one minute each. Scrape down the sides of the bowl before adding the next egg. Once all of the eggs have been added, beat on medium speed for an additional minute.

7. Add half of the dry ingredients, mixing until just combined. Add all of the liquid, mixing until combined, then the remainder of the dry ingredients. (Like cleaning fine china, be gentle, but thorough with your mixing. You can continue on with the electric mixer, but I usually use a whisk or rubber spatula at this point to avoid overmixing. You don't want to see any spots of flour, but you don't want to go so stir-crazy— bad joke, I know—that the cake ends up tough as rubber.)

8. Pour the batter into the prepared pan. Smooth the top and tap the pan on a hard surface to make sure the batter is distributed evenly and there are no huge air bubbles hiding out. Slide into the hot oven and bake for 30–35 minutes, or until a toothpick inserted in the center comes out clean or with one or two crumbs attached.

9. Cool in the pan for 10 minutes, then gently run an offset spatula or butter knife around the cake, pressing against the pan to avoid collateral cake damage. Turn the cake onto a rack to cool completely, parchment side down. Once it is cool, remove and discard the parchment.

Serve deliciously plain, topped with a drizzle of cold cream, or dusted with a little powdered sugar. Sunday Cake stays lovely for a few days if kept wrapped in plastic at room temperature. Tightly wrapped in plastic and foil, it will keep for a few months in the freezer.

WHAT WOULD JOAN JETT DO?

Who's your idol—your favorite writer, human rights leader, comedian, friend? What do you imagine that person does to be happy? Write it here.

Ask your friends to make goofy faces, take a picture, and paste them here.

EMAIL SCRAPBOOK

Print out your favorite emails and save them here. Maybe it's a message from your brother, telling you how your niece talked about you during her Show-and-Tell session. Or perhaps you want to save the email from your boss in which he praises your insight and persistence in finishing a particularly difficult project. And of course, you'll want to save the sweet flirty emails from your crush or love notes from your significant other.

GOOD AND CRABBY

Sometimes, when you're having a super bad day, happy is the last thing you want to focus on. That's OK. Here's a page for you to let your inner crabby out, to get the badness of your bad day out of your system and to list all your pet peeves, no matter how arbitrary they are. Run with it. Relish it. Release it.

MAKE YOUR OWN SILVER LINING

Now that you've had your crabby moment, here's the time to take that clichéd advice—"Every cloud has a silver lining"—and push it to the extreme. What cruddy things happened to you that led to who you are today? What silver lining came from bad things? What good things might come out of your bad day?

*Bonus: Track down a silver pen and fill in this page with silver thoughts.

HAPPY BOOK BOOK LOG

What books make you happy? Keep track of them here. Make your friends and family read them. Become an overzealous book recommender.

Spontaneous Happiness Generator!

Watching the August meteor shower in the Adirondacks.
Tara

The first snowfall of the year makes me happy.
That, and my friends!
Judi

Opening Day at Yankee Stadium — Fritz

Coconut cupcakes. They always look like they're
ready for a party. — Jessica

Lying on the ground, and staring at the moon
and stars. — Kerry

A baby belly-giggling — Judy

AMELIE'S GNOME

Need a reason to take some goofy pictures? We've got one. Whether you travel for work or for fun, don't ever go alone. Bring along your own personal mascot (homemade or store-bought), and take goofy pictures of him wherever you go.

Mascot in the board room! Mascot on the Jersey Shore! Mascot in first class! It's hard not to be happy when you're snapping a picture of your stuffed unicorn taking a subway ride or your Blythe doll in front of the Great Pyramid. Include your favorite photos here.

For inspiration, search "Flat Stanley" on Flickr.com.

THE POSTCARD PROJECT

The last postcard I received was from my mom. It said, "It's hot," and featured a bland photo of the New Mexico landscape on the flip side. Still, I got a rush when I spotted a postcard in my mailbox.

—Rachel

Use postcards for good and send them to someone who needs them. Soldiers in Iraq. Seniors in a nursing home. Friends who need a pick-me-up. If you're crafty, decorate a bunch of blank postcards—they're pennies a piece at any craft or stationery store. If not, find a design you like and make the message your own. Favorite quotes, jokes, random facts, or just a simple earnest "Someone's thinking of you" could turn someone's day from awful to extraordinary.

Some ideas for spreading the postcard love:

- Check in with your local nursing home and see if they're open to passing out some happy greetings to seniors without a network of friends and family.
- Visit Postcrossing.com where you can sign up to send and receive postcards from all over the world.
- If you have a niece or other special little friend, send them a knock-knock joke via postcard every Monday of the year. Or a silly science fact. Or a tongue twister. Kids love getting mail!
- AnySoldier.com puts folks in touch with American soldiers in need of mail, care packages, and good thoughts.

Your Own Happy Pages: Fill in whatever manner you wish.

Last year I started a new tradition with my niece and nephew. On Christmas Eve we assembled a glorious, candy-covered gingerbread house. On New Year's Eve we took the house outside and destroyed it with rocks and a toy hammer. Making the house was fun. Destroying the house was exhilarating!

—*Rachel*

Now it's time for you to make your own mess—here are some ideas to get you started. When you're done, take a picture and paste it in here.

- Bake cookies with a friend and have a flour fight. Don't worry about the kitchen, you can clean it later.
- Build a sandcastle. Make it beautiful. Them stomp on it until it turns back into shapeless sand.
- Cover your kitchen table with a plastic tablecloth. Dump a bowl of pudding on the table and start finger-painting.

Scouts shouldn't be the only ones to earn merit badges. Choose to learn a few new skills (sample sale survival badge!) or to accomplish a few new things (eat ice cream for dinner!). Fill in the blank badges below and crow about them!

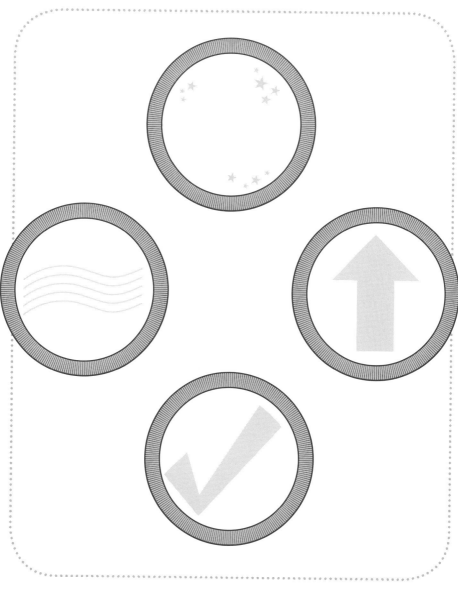

HOT CHOCOLATE.
HOT CHOCOLATE.
HOT CHOCOLATE.

HOT CHOCOLATE WITH
MARSHMALLOWS.

I'm a productivity junkie. I use all kinds of hacks, tricks, and tips to organize my work life and home life. And that got me to thinking… why not subvert some of those hacks for happy means? Here are a few ideas I've put into practice.

—Rachel

- Keep a list of happy blogs on your RSS reader. At the top of my list is BoingBoing.net, one of the smartest, happiest, prettiest sites in the universe. Some of my other sites include: My Paper Crane, Cute Overload, I Can Has Cheezburger, and Wish Jar Journal.
- Stop being so practical about your Delicious bookmarks and start tagging things that make you happy. Keep it nice and general (tag happy things "happy") or break it down into categories ("catsinhats" or "ninjas" or "cake"). Visit your happy-tagged spots when you're feeling crummy.
- Send yourself good thoughts. Set your Outlook or Google calendar to give you some good news each morning. I love being greeted at 8:59 a.m. with the message, "You look so pretty today!" Sure, I told the computer to tell me I look pretty, but it makes me happy regardless.
- Start a blog of happy things. Sites like Tumblr make it quick and painless to start a site where you can keep images, videos, links, and text files. Use it for things that would be hard to track in your happy book.

DOROTHY'S SHOES

Think of Dorothy in *The Wizard of Oz*—she simply had to put on ruby red slippers and click her heels three times to find what she loved best: home. What are your favorite shoes? When did you get them? Why do you love them so much? Write about those shoes that made you happy and paste in a picture of you sporting those kicks or draw them below.

TIME MACHINE

On your birthday (or any day), make a list about where you're at right now. What are you listening to on your iPod? Who are you spending time with? What great book did you just read? Now seal it up in an envelope and tuck it away in a place you can't easily get to it, (for example, taping it to the far inner corner of your closet). A year later, open it. Revel in how you've changed or stayed the same—and then start writing yourself another letter for next year. Make it a tradition, and reread the accumulated letters every year.

If you're the patient type, consider waiting more than a year to read the accumulated letters—maybe read them on every fifth or tenth birthday.

Consider including the following:

- Date
- Current weather
- The specific items of clothing you're wearing
- Your current most-played iPod songs
- The most recent movie you've seen
- The most recent movie you've loved
- What just happened on your favorite television show
- Who you're currently in love with
- What you wish you could own right now
- Your next vacation destination
- What you're currently most worried about
- Your most recent best moment
- Your wishes for the upcoming year

BLOW BUBBLES

Back in grad school, I would blow bubbles (inside my studio apartment—bad idea) when I was having a bad day.

—Rachel

Go out and get yourself some bubble solution, find a stoop or a bench, and blow away. Use this space to write about it.

BE A CURATOR OF HAPPY

Curate your own art collection, right in this book. Find pictures and post-cards and re-create your favorite pieces of art here—you know, the pieces that fill you with awe (Vincent van Gogh's *La Nuit Étoilée, Arles*) and wonder (Gaudí's Sagrada Familia), the pieces that provoke you (Jenny Holzer's aphorisms) and fill you with joy (pretty much anything by Miró), and the pieces that inspire you to be an artist yourself (Rob Ryan's gorgeous cut-outs). You can also add other types of art, from your favorite cartoon to a magazine photo that catches your eye.

RECIPE FOR CHEERING UP A FRIEND

One of the tiny miracles that comes from being surprised is forgetting your current conscious self, even if just for a few minutes. If you have a friend who needs some small moment of stepping outside of herself, this activity harnesses the gift of surprise to create that very effect.

What you need:

- Envelopes: big ones, small ones, colored ones, white ones
- Markers
- Odd pieces of stationery—all the leftover stuff you keep saving
- Other assorted supplies, as your imagination dictates

Your goal here is to fill a set of envelopes with surprises and delights. Be as random as possible when gathering your materials. Some ideas:

- $3 to buy an ice cream cone
- A copy of the children's book *Alexander and the Terrible, Horrible, No Good, Very Bad Day*, by Judith Viorst (a supremely comforting misery-loves-company read, no matter how old you are)
- A funny cartoon (try *The Far Side* to get started)
- Well wishes you've solicited from mutual friends
- A hand-designed bookmark with reading suggestions
- A ready-made grocery list and instructions to make homemade soup
- A lucky smashed penny
- A mix of happy songs

Once you've gathered your supplies, put them in the envelopes, along with notes (written with colorful markers, of course) providing instructions: "Use this $3 to buy an ice cream cone right now."

Give the packet to your friend with instructions to open an envelope whenever it's needed. Don't explain any more than that—you're giving your friend the gift of surprise.

To celebrate the hilarity that is *The Office*, NBC recently offered a shirt that commemorated the quirky goodness of Dwight Schrute. It simply stated Dwight's three favorite things: Beets, Bears, *Battlestar Galactica*. There was something so perfect about that shirt that I bought one for Meg and one for me.

—*Rachel*

The things that make you happiest might be a little weird. Triple-cream goat cheese and Columbus Day? Natural history museums, kitten ears, and IKEA? Like snowflakes and fingerprints, everyone's happy formula is completely unique. There's no need to keep your happy formula secret—wear it on your chest! Here's what you need to do:

1. Give yourself five minutes to write down all the things that make you smile.
2. Choose the three things on the list that you just can't live without.
3. Head out to your nearest craft store and buy a blank shirt, iron-on letters, puffy paint—whatever you need to express your joy. And list the things on your shirt!

(Or, for a quick fix, check out the folks at neighborhoodies.com or zazzle.com, who can do the work for you.)

Falling in love can be heady and scary, but also marvelous. List the first kisses and first dates, the meetings of like minds that made and still make you happy.

"Every relationship has at least one really good day. What I mean is, no matter how sour things go, there's always that day. That day is always in your possession. That's the day you remember. You get old and you think: well, at least I had that day. It happened once. You think all the variables might just line up again. But they don't. Not always. I once talked to a woman who said, 'Yeah, that's the day we had an angel around.'"

—*Charles Baxter,* The Feast of Love

Fun acrostics are a vital part of elementary school life.

So here's what you're going to do. Use this page to make acrostics of your name, your friend's name, your cat's name—go acrostic crazy. You remember acrostics, right? It's when the first letter of each line spells out another word. We'll get you started with the happiest of happy acronyms:

> **H**elium balloon bunches
> **A**mbling through the park
> **P**eople watching on a Sunday
> **P**uppies in a basket
> **Y**arn balls and kittens

In *My Life in France*, Julia Child writes about living in Marseille. She says, "That night we stayed up past midnight writing letters while just below our window a tugboat went *choopa-choopa-choopa-choopa*." What noises do you hear around you? Record them here. Try to capture the noises in words.

Who do you want to thank? It doesn't just have to be for birthday gifts. Who gave you a compliment when you really needed to hear something nice? Left a cookie on your desk? Bought you a copy of your favorite comic book? List those people and their gifts here. Then, spend a few hours composing unexpected but deserved thank-you notes.

"I can no other answer make, but, thanks, and thanks."

—*William Shakespeare*

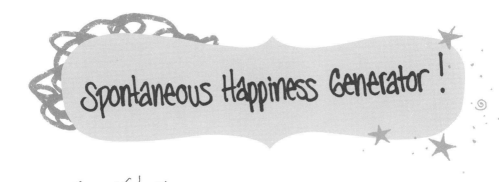

Spontaneous Happiness Generator!

Grocery Shopping
Playing online poker
Winning at online poker
Playing with my children
Going out with My Wife —Donovan

playing Guitar Hero. ——Sean

Clean white sheets, new episodes of Deadliest Catch, a full glass of red wine... all in the same night. —Nancy E.

Eating a chocolate macaron... in Paris.
—Jenny

The smell of the first snowfall of the year. —Michelle

Driving with the windows down (and the music up!) on that first sweet warm day in spring ~ Peg

Let your inner cheerleader out by attending an event where you can cheer people on—a marathon, sports game, or a parade will do the trick. Cheer with abandon and let yourself become a super fan! Write about the experience.

For my eighteenth birthday, my grandma and grandpa booked me passage on a hot air balloon. I hadn't asked for such a present, and I was deathly afraid of heights. I dreaded it for months. But there was no turning back, and the next thing you know I was floating over Arizona in a wicker basket under the biggest, brightest, rainbow-colored balloon I'd ever seen. It was a remarkable way to usher in adulthood, and I'm happy I did it—but I will never ever ever do that again.

—*Rachel*

What have you accomplished that you're glad you never, ever have to do again? Make a list here, and write why you're glad you're done with those things. Think big (finished my dissertation!) and small (tried eel!).

Paste the labels of your favorite candies here. Doodle and reflect about all your happiest candy memories—from your first Sour Patch Kid to your most recent Snickers bar.

HIDDEN TREASURES

Meg and I like *Amelie* a lot—can you tell? The film is set in motion when Amelie finds a box of hidden childhood treasures in her apartment. The thrill of hiding things and finding things makes life more magical, no?

—*Rachel*

Make someone's life a little more wondrous by engaging in a little subterfuge:

- Tape your favorite poem on the telephone poles around town.
- Leave a paperback book that you loved at your local coffee shop (investigate bookcrossing.com for more inspiration).
- Write a note to a friend on the door of a bathroom stall…and see how long it takes them to notice it.
- Write a happy greeting to a stranger on the door of a public bathroom stall.

TRU LUV 4-EVER!!!!!!!!!!!

Who do you love best? Who's your crush? Give free reign to your giddy school kid and fill the page with "tru luv" doodles. You know the type: hearts with arrows through them, your initials, writing your "married" name (new last name or hyphenated!). Draw the person, list your first dance at your wedding, imagine your future home and kids, create a "Do you like me? Check here" box…whatever gets your heart stirring. Use lots of exclamation points and abbreviations.

"It's a perfect day for making out."

—*The Cure*

What will you be doing five years from now? Use the prompts of social networking to look into the future and see your happy future self.

Life Update:.................................... is ....

....

Quote: ....

....

Personal Information: ....

....

....

Activities: ....

....

....

Interests: ....

....

....

About Me: ....

....

....

School/Work: ....

....

....

Clubs: ....

....

....

Member of: ....
Friends: ....

....

....

Influences: ....

....

....

Comments: ....

....

....

In college, a sweet southern-accented boy named Ryan once said to me, "Even though I just met you, I'd do anything for you, short of smokin' someone." This was, hands-down, the nicest thing anyone had ever said to me, up until recently, when my four-year-old niece, distraught over a flight delay that postponed my visit by a day longer than expected, said, "Aunt Meg, I was so sad, I couldn't finish my chicken nuggets." It is really good to know you're loved.

— *Meg*

What are the nicest things people have said or done for you? Write them here.

Your Own Happy Pages: Fill in whatever manner you wish.

Volunteering is one of the happiest things you can do, whether it's helping out at a soup kitchen, cleaning cages at an animal shelter, sorting baby clothes at a women's services organization, or even helping out at a sea turtle sanctuary in Costa Rica. You're busy, sure, but spend an hour giving kittens some love and you'll forget all about the TPS reports. They'll be there tomorrow. For now, there's kittens. Track your volunteer projects here.

Remember the best presents you've ever gotten? Keep track of 'em above.

Make up your own holiday, just for kicks. First Kiss Friday? All-Day Movie Day? Ice Cream Tuesday? Now celebrate. Take the day off. Ask your boss now. Don't renege on yourself, don't reschedule—just do it—and write all about your day here.

What are your favorite ice cream flavors? List them here.
Then, plan a night when you will eat a bite (or more) of every single one. Invite friends over for a tasting.

List all your favorite dance songs here. Ask your friends to tell you their favorite dance songs. Add them to the list. Put them all on your iPod for those days when you need to boogie yourself to work. Make a mix. Dance.

When's the last time you belly laughed? What made you laugh so hard?

"Life is worth living as long as there's a laugh in it."

—L. M. Montgomery, Anne of Green Gables

One summer, I saw my one-and-a-half-year-old nephew actually shiver with excitement when he was handed a banana to eat. It reminded me of being a kid and trying to fall asleep the night before my family left for vacation. I'd lie in bed and try to calm down, so I wouldn't be tired the next day, but I couldn't calm down—even my bones were excited.

— *Meg*

What made you hyper with excitement as a kid? What things did you anticipate with every eager bone in your body?

Eat like a little kid for an entire day. Sugar cereal and donuts for breakfast. Peanut butter and jelly on white bread, ants on a log (celery sticks with peanut butter and raisins) or apple slices for lunch. Mac and cheese with chocolate milk for dinner. And don't forget to break for fruit snacks and Pop-Tarts!

Plan your perfect kid's day menu.

Look out this window. What do you want to see? Draw it or collage it or write it.

Our friend Michelle throws lovely themed parties: British Invasion (we all had to dress up as characters from the UK), International Bazaar (we all had to bring food from another country), Red Birthday (all food, costumes, and lighting were red, for our friend's birthday). Carry on by throwing a theme party of your own. Celebrate something that makes you happy—pie, the movies of Baz Lurhmann, Vivaldi's *Four Seasons*, Britney's greatest hits. Document your parties here.

Your Own Happy Pages: Fill in whatever manner you wish.

THE WISH NECKLACE

Blowing out birthday candles, seeing a falling star, and finding an eyelash shouldn't be the only occasions you get to wish. It's time to reclaim the power of wish-making by making a wish necklace.

What you'll need:

- Some silk cord (available in the jewelry section of your local craft store)
- A charm (craft stores sell inexpensive gold and silver charms—but we'll also tell you how to make your own)
- A wish

For the make-your-own charm:

- Shrink paper (a thin plastic sheet that shrinks in a super cool way when you bake it; you can find shrink paper online or at craft stores)
- Colored pencils
- A hole punch
- A cookie sheet
- Silk cording

You can find pre-made charms at jewelry supply stores, bead shops, or even from a bubblegum machine. Now add a length of silk cording (big enough so you can easily slip it over your head), knot it, and you're set.

If you don't want to buy a charm, you can make your own using shrink paper. Decide on a simple shape (shrink paper is awesome, but not great for detail unless you've got a knack for it). Trace the design onto the shrink paper, and then color the nonshiny side using colored pencils. Cut the pattern out and punch a hole out for your cord. Follow the shrink paper package instructions and bake your charm in the oven. Watch it shrink—feel the love! When your charm is out of the oven and cooled, string it onto your cord.

As you place the necklace over your head, make a wish.

Wear the necklace every day, until the cord breaks. Some say that when the cord breaks and the charm falls off, your wish will come true. Even if it doesn't, you've got a new necklace and a great party conversation starter.

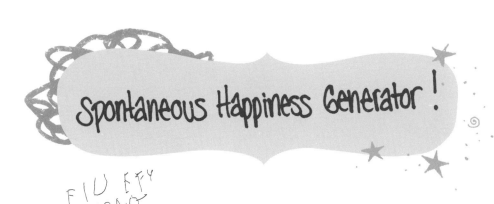

Spontaneous Happiness Generator!

FIU ETY
DA NANO
PRINCESSES
FAIRIES
De io ner

Sitting around a fire gazing at a starry sky ~Becky

Grandkids in front of the fireplace on
cold Sunday afternoons
                              Tom

A long run on a beautiful fall day – Anna

daily good morning text messages from my father. –– Sonya

Watching episodes of "Hey Dude" on my
iphone during my train commute.
                              – Melinda F.

BREAK-TIME HAPPY OLYMPICS

Need a break? Here's a list of things you can do to amuse yourself in a flash when you're studying or toiling away at the office. Try them, then add your own ideas to the list.

- Staple your name onto a piece of paper. It's kind of impossible, but endlessly amusing.
- Start a rubber band ball.
- Build a robot using only Scotch tape, coffee cups, and paperclips.
- Invite in some friends, shut your office door, turn on some music, and hold a five-minute dance party.
- Use your label maker for good, not evil. Print up some labels with silly or sweet sayings and stick them in surprising places around your officemates' desks.
- Redecorate your office door or cubicle wall.
- Test out all the pens, pencils, and markers lingering around your desk. Throw away the writing implements that displease you.
- Find a terrible piece of clip art and give it a nutty caption.
- Make a PowerPoint presentation that extols your love of something silly. Like cabbage. Or *Futurama*.
- Keep track of your lunches and then display your results in a pie chart at the end of each week.
- Hold a secret cupcake party for the co-workers you like. Don't let office politics interfere with your guest list.
- Doodle your co-workers' faces during boring meetings.
- Send your next email as a pictogram.
- Make yourself and your co-workers spiffy new name placards.
- Bring in real marshmallows, cinnamon, flavored creamers—anything that will improve your normal 3 p.m. coffee break.
- Create an office-specific crossword puzzle. You can find free crossword puzzle makers all over the Internet (I did this for a co-worker's birthday and it was shockingly fun—Rachel).

Fill this page with stickers!

If you had unlimited time and resources, what would be your perfect road trip? A tour of the best pie-serving diners in the United States? A trip to Graceland with a stop for ribs at The Rendezvous? Going up the coastline of the Pacific Northwest? Driving across Ireland from Dublin to the Dingle Peninsula? Plan out your dream trip and paste a copy of the route here. List the perfect road trip music mix. Brainstorm on your ideal travel companion.

> "Most of us can remember a time when a birthday—especially if it was one's own—brightened the world as if a second sun has risen."
>
> —Robert Lynd

To put it quite simply, birthdays rock! What was your best birthday? Flavor of cake? Attendees? Write all your favorite birthday memories here.

Start a collection of odd things that make you happy—plastic deer figurines, smashed pennies from tourist sites, Bazooka Joe comics. It can be a collection of all one thing (you'll become the plastic deer buyer all other eBay collectors fear!) or a collection of odd knick-knacks you just like (a giant pencil from Niagara Falls, a rock that looks like gold). Document your collection here.

A VERY MERRY UN-BIRTHDAY

One year for our shared birthdays, my friend Megan and I threw a rocking roller-skating party. The next year, we decided we'd have to figure out something pretty spectacular to match the previous shindig. Both fans of *Through the Looking Glass*, we decided to throw an un-birthday party.

When our friends arrived at the bar for the celebration, they found cupcakes and a multitude of wrapped presents—all for them, from us. We also gave presents to the other patrons, to the bartender, to the cook. The presents were simple—tchotchkes from the thrift store, a garden gnome, Japanese candy—but none were for the birthday girls. And it was, in a word, awesome. We were birthday queens, bestowing presents upon all our un-birthday friends.

— *Meg*

For your next birthday, throw an un-birthday party. Don't tell your friends what it entails—just invite them to be at a certain place at a certain time. And then, give them gifts, give them cake, tell them you love them.

How to throw an un-birthday party:

1. It's best to throw an un-birthday party on your actual birthday. Tell your friends to keep that day open.
2. Gather a bunch of unexpected but lovely items—a mini box of Lucky Charms cereal, gumball machine prizes, a mix of soft rock songs, a box of cool fossils—and wrap them.
3. Make some cupcakes, preferably with sprinkles. Maybe they will have pink icing.
4. Invite your friends to meet somewhere.

5. When they get there, yell, "Happy un-birthday!"
6. Let them pick a gift from the mountain of presents.
7. Share the cupcakes.
8. Refuse any gifts offered to you…after all, it's your birthday, not your un-birthday.

"I mean, what *is* an un-birthday present?"
"A present given when it isn't your birthday, of course."
Alice considered a little. "I like birthday presents best," she said at last.
"You don't know what you're talking about!" cried Humpty Dumpty.
"How many days are there in a year?"
"Three hundred and sixty-five," said Alice.
"And how many birthdays have you?"
"One."

—*Lewis Carroll*, Through the Looking Glass

Fill this page with all the smiles you can find. Take pictures of people's smiles (just the smiles!), collect smiles from magazines, draw your own…whatever you need to do to make this wall-to-wall happy.

List the top three funniest things you've ever seen firsthand.

Strap on a camera, plot out a course, and be a tourist for a day! There's nothing not to love about being a tourist—you can gawk with abandon, eat taffy and fudge, and forget about the stresses of everyday work and life. And the best part? You can experience that glorious feeling of abandon without leaving town. Find completely ridiculous, off-the-beaten trail things to do—locate the largest local collection of taxidermied and costumed squirrels, the biggest ball of yarn, or the restaurant with blue-ribbon borscht. Eat something strange you haven't tried before, order ice cream in the dead of winter, or spend $2 on a single decadent piece of chocolate. Record your adventures here:

Travel Date:

I Saw:

I Ate:

Tourist Photos:

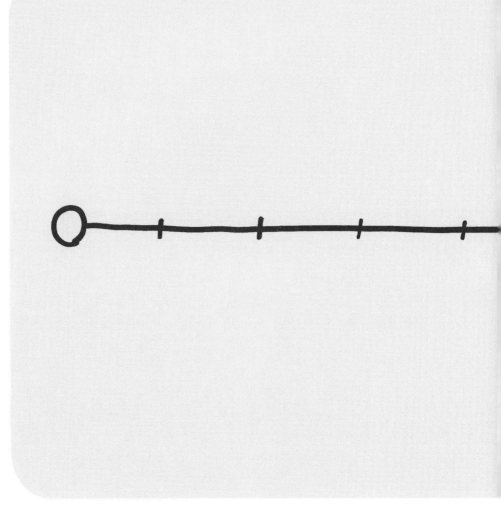

YOUR HAPPY TIMELINE

Use these pages to plot the best times of your life, big and small. When did you learn how to ride a bike? Get your first business card? Hold your new-born nephew? Start when you were born (because that was your first happy day!) and add from there.

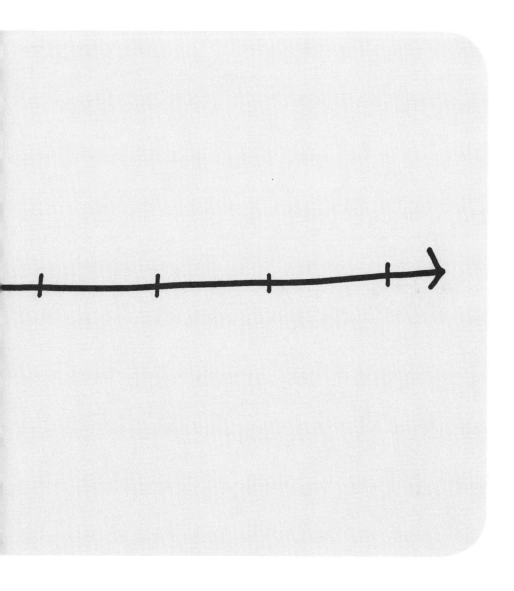

Taking classes is fun! Sign up for a class on wine tasting, crocheting, ceramic painting, hip-hop dancing—anything that will bring a new kind of joy to your everyday life. Write about your experience here and paste in some mementos from your class (your first knitting swatch, the name of the first song you danced to, etc.).

"Isn't it splendid to think of all the things there are to find out about? It just makes me feel glad to be alive—it's such an interesting world."

—*L. M. Montgomery,* Anne of Green Gables

WHEN HOBBIES ATTACK

Sometimes hobbies turn stressful. If you took up knitting to relax, only to saddle yourself with an unmanageable to-do list of Christmas projects, knitting becomes a great big chore. Same goes for those of us engaged in any creative pursuit, from writing to crafting to drawing to making music.

So do yourself a happy favor, and use this space to write about why the *process* of creating is something you love. And then commit to spending at least an hour a day working on something just for the joy of doing it.

Which of your friends have the most infectious laugh? Write about it.

Fill in your name below, and then ask your friends and family to write fill-in-the-blanks on this page. Consider it an instant pick-me-up you can always pick up.

[Your name here]

rocks because...

Host a meeting of like minds. Find something you're passionate about—talking about the best episodes of *Buffy the Vampire Slayer* and *Lost*, the simple movements involved in knitting, watching old John Hughes movies, the world's greatest figure skaters, playing old board games—and find friends and friends of friends who share your passion. Organize a regular gathering to share in the joy of what you love. Make it as formal or informal as you wish. You may want to have discussion topics and presentations (a demonstration of a new crafting technique, a PowerPoint presentation of what you love about *Friday Night Lights*), or you may simply want to gather in a home or café and talk about what you love. Regardless, make sure you come up with a name for your group—TV Night, The Secret Cocktail Society, Craft Monday—and document your group's history here: charter members, founding date, what you all love most about what you're sharing.

Make some bread. Kneading is a stress-buster and freshly baked bread cures even the crabbiest of moods. Try out a few different recipes, and paste your favorite one here.

"If thou tastest a crust of bread, thou tastest all the stars and all the heavens."

—Robert Browning

STAR GAZING

These are your pages for star gazing. Fill them with gold stars like the ones teachers give out, stars cut out from aluminum foil, any constellations you create. Look for stars when you're out and about—they're everywhere…on old barns, brownstones, and in signs. Take pictures of them and paste them here. Collect them for wishing.

"For my part I know nothing with any certainty, but the sight of the stars makes me dream."

—Vincent van Gogh

Spontaneous Happiness Generator!

The Daily Show, a seat on the train, 8 hours sleep, a perfect landing — and Sydney.

Vicki

My mommy and my daddy.

Sydney

Holding my baby when she sleeps. — Sara

A big cup of coffee and a bran muffin in the morning.
— Michael

Pretending to be a mermaid at the Red Hook pool.
— Donya

When my husband calls me "monkey."

Megan

An afternoon all to myself & its infinite possibilities

Alice

flying home to Florida. Koren

Who do you see everyday, but not really see? Your bus driver, the security guard at your bank, the receptionist at your office, the clerk at your corner deli? Share something happy with that person…from a morning hello for your receptionist to a coffee for the man selling papers at your local newsstand to a four-leaf clover for your bus driver. Keep a record of your happy-spreading efforts here.

"But the world is so full of people, so crowded with these miracles that they become commonplace and we forget…I forget. We gaze continually at the world and it grows dull in our perceptions. Yet seen from another's vantage point, as if new, it may still take the breath away."

—*Alan Moore*, The Watchmen

Come up with a goal, big or small, and celebrate when you hit it. Did you read one hundred books in a year (we did!)? Drop a pants size? Find the prized cookie jar you've sought for years? Write about it.

Our friends Meredith and Lance make up very funny witty words: snain (a mixture of snow and rain), m'pris (Capri pants for men). Do you have words you wish everyone used? List them here.

CUPCAKE CRAWL

Recently, some colleagues at work created a "Cupcake Crawl" for two newly engaged friends. They planned an afternoon of visiting some of the best cupcake bakeries in NYC—Sugarsweet Sunshine, Magnolia, The Cupcake Café, Billy's Bakery, and Crumbs—and provided a highlighted map of instructions.

On this page, map out a cupcake (or pie or sandwich or pizza) crawl, finding the best your town has to offer. Plan a day when you can take your friends on the crawl. Make sure you're good and hungry before you begin. Document your journey here.

A few years ago I fell out of touch with Henni, a dear childhood friend. I felt guilty and terrible, and the more time passed the more guilty and terrible I felt. One night, I decided to just write my friend a letter. Henni was happy to hear from me, and in return she sent me birthday and Christmas cards to make up for the five years we'd been out of touch.

—Rachel

It's easy to lose track of people you love. Even with email and Facebook, some amazing friends can get lost in the rush of everyday life. Now is your chance to change that. Use this page to write about someone special that you've lost touch with over time. If you're feeling brave, seek out your missing piece.

Paste all your favorite ticket stubs on this page.

The art of writing letters is being lost in this age of email and IM-ing. Spend some time writing a letter to someone and then mail it. Here are some ideas to make your letters extra pretty:

- Photocopy a favorite photograph and write your letter on the back.
- Write each paragraph in a different pen color.
- Write a short note to your friend each day for a week. Number the notes, and send them off. Instruct your reader to open a letter a day, and then ask her to repeat the process with you.
- Go rubber stamp crazy and make your own hand-stamped stationary. Even the most no-frills craft store has hundreds of cute and quirky stamps and a rainbow of ink pads. It's crafting at its easiest. Stamp away on this page.
- Doodle like mad! Use the doodle art you find throughout the book as inspiration.

When you're flipping through magazines, what images make you happy? Beautiful flowers? An especially great pair of red cowboy boots? Tear them out and paste them here.

RANDOM ACTS OF KINDNESS

There's an insurance commercial that I adore. A man picks up a little girl's doll. Her mom, in turn, helps a man at a coffee shop avoid overturning his coffee mug. The coffee shop man helps a stranger who fell on the sidewalk—and so it goes and goes and goes. Some call it paying it forward, others call it random acts of kindness. I call it pure happy goodness.

—Rachel

Get into the practice of doing small, kind things every month or every week or every day. Log them here.

Date:
What I Did:

Why It Made Me Happy:

Date:
What I Did:

Why It Made Me Happy:

Date:
What I Did:

Why It Made Me Happy:

Date:
What I Did:

Why It Made Me Happy:

RANDOM ACTS OF "KIDNESS"

Kids do things adults don't do: they make snow angels, catch lightning bugs, skip cracks on the sidewalk, draw sidewalk murals, spontaneously run for no reason, twirl in circles. What things do you no longer do, now that you're "grown up"? List them here. Then try some of them again.

Your Own Happy Pages: Fill in whatever manner you wish.

"Man is fond of counting his troubles, but he does not count his joys. If he counted them up as he ought to, he would see that every lot has enough happiness provided for it."

—Fyodor Dostoevsky

GUERRILLA HAPPINESS

Gather index cards and under the header, "These things make me happy," write short lists of random items that make you happy. Or copy the cards on the next page, fill them out with your ideas, cut them out, and start distributing! Do not sign them. Post them in the following places:

- Community bulletin boards at your coffee shop, grocery store, or food co-op
- Above the sink at your workplace
- On the back of the seat in front of you on the bus
- On a lamppost

Reasons why life is pretty dang cool:

Terrible day? Instead, think about:

Seven reasons to be happy:
1.
2.
3.
4.
5.
6.
7.

Finish this book the way you started…listing the things that make you happy. Onward!

"The essentials to happiness are something to love, something to do, and something to hope for."

—William Blake

This is the happiest book in the world. For days or weeks or months you filled it with wonderful thoughts and notes and photos and other souvenirs of happiness. You took the time to explore, to record, and to examine happy things of all kinds. You took goofy pictures, looked into the future, baked a yummy cake, and gave a helping hand to a stranger. You recorded all your favorite lines from your favorite books, spread cheer to sad friends, and spent a day drinking juice boxes and munching on tater tots. And now you're finished, so let's mark the occasion:

Today, on the _____ day of _____

in the year _____,

_____

finished *The Happy Book*.

Congratulations! You did it! And now it's time to celebrate by starting up a new happy book.

What? It's not over? No way! Meg has five happy books. Rachel has two, and by the time you read this she'll be working through her third. You've got your happy book chops, and now it's time for you to continue with your sequel. Head out there into the world and buy yourself a journal or a notebook. Maybe you'll use it to keep a never-ending list of happy things (like Meg) or a nutsy hybrid scrapbook (like Rachel). Or maybe you'll pick your favorite activities from *The Happy Book* and keep doing them over and over and over. Keep doing this—keep focusing on the ladybug that lands on your arm, noticing the smiles of your favorite people, dancing to "Doing The Unstuck," sharing cookies with your postman, leaving notes taped to park benches for friends, planning magical dinner parties, and staring out windows full of possibility.

Yours in happiness,

Meg Leder

Rachel Kempster

acknowledgments

Thank you to Shana Drehs and Michael Bourret for liking our book and making it better.

Thank you to Jessica Reed for Cake Thursday and Sunday Cake.

Thank you to our friends, family, and favorites for sharing what makes them happy and for awesome doodles.

about the authors

Meg is an editor who lives in Brooklyn, NY. These things make her happy: Sharpies, Pie Day, her cat Baxter, talking about sci-fi with her dad, kickboxing, reading, and Skyline Chili. And stars.

Rachel is a book publicist who lives in Astoria, NY. These things make her happy: her friends, cat hats, unicorns, tv, stacks of books, robots, yarn, and the Blue Ribbon Bakery.

Goodbye!